A Special Gift

*For*_____

From _____

*Date*_____, 19 _____

Flowers for Mother

Flowers for Mother

LEROY BROWNLOW

Brownlow Publishing Company, Inc.

Brownlow Gift Books

A Father's World

A Few Hallelujahs for Your Ho-Hums

A Psalm in My Heart

As a Man Thinketh

Better Than Medicine—A Merry Heart

Children Won't Wait

Flowers for Mother

Flowers for You

Flowers of Friendship

Flowers That Never Fade

For Mom With Love

Give Us This Day

Grandpa Was a Preacher

Great Verses of the Bible

It's a One-derful Life

Jesus Wept

Just Between Friends

Leaves of Gold

Making the Most of Life

The Fruit of the Spirit

The Greatest Thing in the World

Thoughts of Gold—Wisdom for Living

Today and Forever

Today Is Mine

University of Hard Knocks

Contents

	Foreword	6
I.	Honor to Whom Honor Is Due	9
II.	Home Is Where Mother Is	15
III.	"The Hand That Rocks the Cradle"	21
IV.	My Mother	27
V.	A Mother's Love	30
VI.	Rock Me to Sleep	37
VII.	Mother and Prayer	40
VIII.	A Priceless Mother	46
IX.	The Brave Mother	56
X.	A Prayer for Mothers	62

Foreword

GIVING FLOWERS to those we love is a beautiful custom. Flowers are the delicate and exquisite materialization of God's love. As a token of His care, He has woven them as embroidery in nature's garments. They decorate the world in the most gorgeous clothing to greet the eye of man. On bowing stems and waving branches, God has hung the crimson hues and the snowy white blossoms as a reminder of His feeling for us. Being the offspring of God and drawn by the divine instinct, it is natural that we, too, seek a token of affection which we may give to those we love.

These are the flowers of thought which have sprung from the heart-soil of sons and daughters and husbands for centuries. The author has merely expressed these flower-thoughts in words which convey our appreciation of mother and our devotion to her. They are flowers— thoughts—plucked from our hearts and laid upon hers. They are our precious feelings of gratitude to mother.

As Solomon said, "Her children arise up, and call her blessed; her husband also, and he praiseth her" (Proverbs 31:28).

It is also hoped that the fragrance of these flowers may bring a sweetness to the lives of her sons and daughters. Just a remembrance of lofty ideals will bless them. Coleridge said, "Memory is the bosom spring of joy." Ideals shape the destiny of nations as they mold the characters of its citizens.

May these flowers—words—strengthen our homes throughout the world. If they inspire the mothers of today and the young girls, the mothers of tomorrow, to aspire to the most effectual and noblest motherhood, then we have made a contribution to the happiness of the individual, the stability of the home and the future of our civilization. The strength of any country is found in its homes and not in its boarding-houses. The ties of home are the strongest and most sacred of any on earth. Earth's inhabitants go rushing on in their work during the day; but when "fast falls the eventide," the heart is apt to wander back to the protection and security of the home.

This feeling holds our society together.

The hope is now entertained that *Flowers for Mother* may help to perpetuate this memory and strengthen those ties which keep our world from breaking apart.

LEROY BROWNLOW

The Watcher

She always leaned to watch for us,
Anxious if we were late,
In winter by the window,
In summer by the gate;

And though we mocked her tenderly,
Who had such foolish care,
The long way home would seem more safe
Because she waited there.

Her thoughts were all so full of us,
She never could forget!
And so I think that where she is
She must be watching yet,

Waiting till we come home to her,
Anxious if we are late—
Watching from Heaven's window,
Leaning from Heaven's gate.

—MARGARET WIDDEMER

1

Honor to Whom Honor Is Due

THE HOLY SCRIPTURES TELL US: "Render therefore to all their dues: tribute to whom tribute is due...honor to whom honor" (Romans 13:7). While this passage is found in the context of paying honor to civil servants, we feel that it contains a principle of life that is applicable to all persons worthy of recognition; and no one is more deserving of honor than honorable parents.

• *The first commandment with promise is to honor father and mother.* "Children, obey your parents in the Lord: for this is right. Honor thy father and mother; which is the first commandment with promise; that it may be well with thee, and thou mayest live long on the earth" (Ephesians 6:1-3). There are many reasons for honoring mother, but of course, the greatest is that the Heavenly Father enjoined it as a sacred commandment upon the children of the race. God saw the need for it in preserving our society. Animals do not honor their mothers, but we are not animals. As human beings created in the divine image of God, we belong to a higher world and are expected to live on the higher plane of humanity. Of course, for a mother to receive the greatest honor, she must be honorable; and for her to receive the greatest praise, she must be praiseworthy. This is understandable and implied.

• *We honor our mothers because we owe to them our lives.* We are blood of their blood, flesh of their flesh and bone of their bone. At travail of body and anxiety of mind, they have made our lives possible. Through their sacrifices we have been given life. This is obvious, but it is also obvious that in the stress and strain of our society we are in danger of forgetting or, at least, neglecting this basic principle of progress. Surely the perpetuation of the race in love and honor is the basic service upon which all future progress depends.

The greatest mission of woman became and is motherhood. In speaking of the first woman, the Bible says, "And Adam called his wife's name Eve; because she was the mother of all living" (Genesis 3:20). In this eminent realm womanhood glorifies God and perpetuates His creation. It is a task that involves a thousand sacrifices, but womanhood with a song on the lips and a prayer in the heart rises triumphantly.

• *We honor mothers because they are our homemakers.* This is God's wise arrangement. Mother is the heartbeat in the home; and without her, there seems to be no heart throb. She is the pulse in the home; and when she is gone, the life current is weak. She is light in the home; and when that light goes out, shadow falls over it. She is life in the home; and when she dies, the home seems dead.

It takes more than architecture to make affection; pictures to make purity; vases to make virtue; and clothes to make character. The wise mother, understanding this, sets her heart and hands to the nobler task of converting a house into a home.

God, in making woman the keeper of the home, extended to her the glory of being the pillars of our society; for the home is truly the foundation of the world. So long as we recognize this sacred thought and hold it dear in our hearts, there is hope for us.

> *So long as we have homes to which men turn*
>   *At close of day;*
> *So long as we have homes where children are*
>   *And women stay;*
> *If love and loyalty and faith be found*
>   *Across those sills,*
> *A stricken nation can recover from*
>   *Its gravest ills.*
>
> —GRACE NOLL CROWELL

• *We honor mothers because they were our first teachers.* From the viewpoint of education and influence, the first few years of our lives are the most important; so we are indebted to mothers for the most vital part of our training. It is then that consideration for the right of others is more easily learned, if ever mastered; then unselfishness is usually acquired, if ever; then obedience is more likely to be learned, if ever learned. In those early years the foundation of character is laid; the disposition is formed; the bent of life is made.

The teachers who impressed us most were not necessarily the instructors with the most intellectual ability, but rather those who had big hearts. Oh, they were smart, but they had more than brilliance. They did something for us that scholarship alone would not produce. They had personalities that reached out and grabbed us, because they had hearts that beat with interest and understanding. They have remained our friends while other teachers have passed out of the range of our lives. It takes a heart to touch a heart. This is why mother remains our favorite teacher.

• *We honor mothers because of their loyalty,* a loyalty so unbreakable that the story of motherhood has come to mean the story of loyalty. When others condemn us, she finds something to praise; when others abandon us, she remains; when others seek to destroy us, she—though weak and feeble—works frantically to save us.

One of the best known examples of maternal loyalty is seen in the life of Mary, the mother of our Lord. As He was being executed on the cross, she came to be with him to the end. "Now there stood by the cross of Jesus his mother"

(John 19:25). No Golgotha's hill is too high for a mother to climb as she walks by the side of her son condemned to die. An army could not keep her away. That is loyalty.

Her love outlasts all other human love,
  Her faith endures the longest, hardest test,
Her tried loyalty through a lifetime proves,
  That she's a friend, the noblest and the best.

• *We can honor mother by providing for her physical care,* if she has need. Jesus did this. His provision for his mother was one of his last earthly acts. It was a touching scene. As our Lord was dying, he made arrangements for John to care for his mother. As all of His deeds were, it was an exemplary act and should be followed by children today. The Bible instructs: "If any man or woman that believeth have widows, let them relieve them, and let not the church be charged" (I Timothy 5:16).

In caring for mother, life has a way of evening up things. When we were young, mother cared for us; now when she is old, we care for her. She fed us; now we feed her. When we were awkward, she loved us; now in her feebleness, she is endeared to us. She watched us get stronger; now we watch her get weaker. Nothing is fairer than this, and nothing can encourage the development of rugged character better than this.

• *We can honor our mothers by loving and petting them now.* They are easy to love, because love begets love. We love them, because they first loved us. In their loneliness, their hearts cry out for affection, and we have the opportunity to supply it.

Love and Pet Me Now

Take my withered hands in yours,
    Children of my soul;
Mother's heart is craving love;
    Mother's growing old.
See, the snows of many years
    Crown my furrowed brow;
As I've loved and petted you,
    Love and pet me now.

Take my withered hands in yours,
    Hold them close and strong;
Cheer me with a fond caress,
    Twill not be for long;
Youth immortal soon will crown
    With its wreath my brow.
As I've loved and petted you,
    Love and pet me now.

—T. B. LARIMORE

2

Home Is Where Mother Is

A CHILD WAS ASKED, "Where is your home?" The little fellow replied, "Where mother is." Ah, that is home— "where mother is." She really makes the home; so where she is, home is. God, having planned for woman to be the keeper of the home, endowed her with special traits which have nobly qualified her for this most strenuous and honorable task. The Bible says she is "to be discreet, chaste, keepers at home" (Titus 2:5).

• *It is in the home that mother gives so much to her children.* What night-watching! what self-denial! what tears! what concern! what joy! what pure love is seen in the home mother makes! She gives the works of her body, the thoughts of her mind and the love of her heart. In her attachment to her children we find all the heights and depths of an undying devotion. It is in the home that these lingering thoughts are written across the heart of the child to remain forever.

• *Home! What a hallowed name mother has made it!* It is full of goodness and sacredness to the heart.

Home is the precious bundle of human ties in which affection has made bonds stronger than iron and where the weak and weary spirit finds strength.

Home! It is the restful asylum to which the careworn soul turns tired steps from the toils and struggles of life.

Home is the fortress in which the tired soldier may confidently shed his armor and find refuge from the "slings and arrows of an outrageous fortune."

Home! It is the name that strikes melody in every fiber of the soul and nothing can stop its music but death.

"Home is the one place in all this world where hearts are sure of each other. It is the place of confidence. It is the place where we tear off that mask of guarded suspiciousness and coldness which the world forces us to wear in self-defense, and where we pour out the unreserved communications of full and confiding hearts. It is the spot where expressions of tenderness flow without any sensation of awkwardness and without any dread of ridicule."—F. W. Robertson.

Home! Even though it was only a humble cabin which never knew a luxury, it is all that we have said about it and a thousand times more; because it was the castle in which mother was the queen. Through the art of living she made a house a home.

If in your case the day of life is nearly spent, it is still a distinct joy to stop and look backward to the old home of your childhood. It is still the home in which mother will always awaken the sweetest memories of life. Time has not dimmed its beauty nor lessened its value. Until we take the last step and pass beyond the realm where earth-time shall be no more, the house mother converted into a home will ever live in our hearts.

• *To mother goes the chief credit for making home a pleasant and happy abode,* because she is the keeper of it. After sixty years of wedded life a husband had this epitaph engraved on the marker at the head of his wife's grave in a little country churchyard: "She always made home happy."

Those who live in houses on hilltops have many more golden hours than those who live in the valleys. It is there that morning comes so early and evening tarries so late. Those who live in the valleys must endure more shadows because the days are shorter and the nights are longer.

From the physical and geographical viewpoint, it is impossible for every house to be located on high ground. But regardless of the location, the loving, efficient mother builds the home on the hilltop of cheerfulness and serenity. She will not permit it to slide between the hills into the valley of discontent and bitterness. She is a light of happiness which drives out any threatening shadows of gloom.

Solomon said:

Every wise woman buildeth her house: but the foolish plucketh it down with her hands.
—*Proverbs 14:1*

• *Home is where mother is,* because of the long hours she works in it. The Bible pays her this immortal tribute: "She riseth also while it is yet night, and giveth meat to her household, and a portion to her maidens" (Proverbs 31:15). It often has been said:

> *A man's work is from sun to sun,*
> *But a mother's work is never done.*

We have read that the thrush goes to work at half-past two every morning during the summer and works until nine-thirty at night—a straight nineteen hours—during which it feeds its young over two hundred times. The blackbird works seventeen hours and feeds its little ones a hundred times a day.

In the home the energetic mother is up early and retires late. Like the hard-working bird, she does it for those who are so precious to her.

• *There is no place like home.* When the toils and cares of the day are over, the children are home from school and the father is home from work and the family circle is once more formed, then you have the most delightful hour. Love sticks out so plainly on everyone that it just rubs off on everyone else; joy so permeates the atmosphere that we are saturated with it; and the strength that each receives from the others gives us all the confidence and assurance of a giant. The world is shut out, and father and mother and children are together in family communion and sacred trust. The perils of life seem removed and there is no fear of evil. Courage is our fortune. The family may be poor, but proud; simple, but sincere. They are several but one, so much united that when one suffers all suffer, and when one rejoices all rejoice. "O Lord, by these things men live." This is home and this is living. This is why:

Mid pleasures and palaces
though we may roam,
Be it ever so humble,
there's no place like home.
—JOHN HOWARD PAYNE

• *In both the saddest and gladdest hours of life the child turns to mother.* Many events which have transpired at death's door illustrate this beautiful thought. This is seen in the following truthful and touching incident:

A little girl, a sweet and precious child, lost her mother at an early age. She was very beautiful, and just as frail. It was easy for her to be the idol of the family and she was, but she was so delicate that life began to fade away early. She would sit upon the lap of a friend who bestowed a mother's kind love upon her; and, reaching one wasted arm around her neck, would say, "Now tell me about my mother." And when the cherished and oft-repeated tale was told, she would softly say, "Take me into the parlor; I want to see my mother." They always took her, and the child with such deep feeling and understanding would lie for hours gazing contentedly on her mother's portrait. Mother was gone, yet she seemed to be there. This gratifying experience enabled the child to feel more keenly her mother's presence and it encouraged her. But—

Pale and wan she grew, and weakly,
Bearing all her pains so meekly,
That to them she still grew dearer,
As the trial-hour grew nearer.

That hour came at last and the loving friends assembled, weeping, going with her as far as they could. But the dew of death had already begun to fall upon the little flower, as life's sun was sinking low. Friends asked, "Do you know me, darling?" But it awoke no answer. As time slipped away, all at once a tiny sparkle of life burst over the child's colorless features. Eyelids with death upon them barely opened and set lips faintly parted, and with one impulsive effort she whispered, "Mother."

Mother is often the first and last word uttered by the child. This is natural, "for out of the abundance of the heart the mouth speaketh" (Matthew 12:34). Mother is endeared to the heart of the child and there are reasons. Mother's love begat love; mother's sacrifice produced appreciation; and mother's heart touched a heart. Inasmuch as home is where the heart is, then we can say, "Home is where mother is."

3

"The Hand that Rocks the Cradle"

*W*HAT A POWER the mother exerts. Her influence is tremendous. She throws a spell around the child which is hard to break.

Largely speaking, the world sees only the son; his name appears in the papers; he receives the glory and honor; but back of his success is that dear mother who exerted a power, who molded a character, who instilled principles in a little heart which made it possible for him to climb. She was the ladder whereby he arose to success.

Queen of Baby Land

*W*ho is queen of baby land?
Mother kind and sweet,
And her love, born above,
Guides the little feet.

• *Mother works with the world's most valuable materi-al:* living beings, little bundles of great possibilities, immortal souls. No workman with gold, silver or precious stones can even begin to approach her in working with values.

Daniel Webster said: "If we work upon marble, it will perish; if we work upon brass, time will efface it; if we rear temples, they will crumble into dust. But if we work upon immortal minds, if we imbue them with high principles, with the just fear of God and love of their fellowmen, we engrave on those tablets something which no time can efface but which will brighten all eternity."

• *The Bible tells of a mother's influence extending from generation to generation.* Paul wrote Timothy: "When I call to remembrance the unfeigned faith that is in thee which dwelt first in thy grandmother Lois, and thy mother Eunice; and I am persuaded that in thee also" (II Timothy 1:5). The holy faith was passed down from mother to the daughter and on to the grandchild. Timothy was supremely blessed in having such a grandmother and mother. It had been his privilege to be taught the Holy Scriptures from a child (II Timothy 3:15). So it is very apparent that the best time to start training a child is with the grandmother.

The mind of the child is pliable and easily affected. This means that mother's responsibility weighs like a mountain upon her, because those first impressions are so effectual.

Everything that is young and tender is easily influenced. Even the tender plants can be directed to grow in any direction. We may take a little bush and apply a weight on the south and it will grow into a tree leaning in that direction. On the other hand, we may apply the weight on the north and it will grow leaning to the north; or we may step on the bush and almost ruin it.

When a thoughtful child was asked why a certain tree in the yard was crooked, he said, "I s'pose somebody must have stepped on it when it was a little fellow."

This principle also holds true of us.

• *This is Solomon's declaration of the power of early influence:* "Train up a child in the way he should go: and when he is old, he will not depart from it" (Proverbs 22:6). If the mother provided for her offspring the childish and youthful memories of restraint, based on righteousness and goodness, they will remain never to be forgotten. It is true that the child may stray from the pathway of right, and may even seem for awhile to have completely forgotten a mother's prayer and a mother's kiss; but, sooner or later, somehow that lovely face and anxious counsel and fond caress will flash upon the mind and, as it does, it will bring with it a power that tugs at the heartstrings and beckons the wayward child to turn backward from ruination.

No doubt thousands of men and women on the brink of temptation have been held back by the hallowed influence thrown around them in early childhood by a great and godly mother.

John Randolph said: "I should have been a French atheist if it had not been for one recollection, and that was that my departed mother used to take my little hand in hers, and cause me, on my knees, to say, 'Our Father which art in heaven....'"

Of all the human names held sacred in memory, that of mother falls upon our hearts with the most sublime influence. How sweet in after years are the recollections of a mother's patient training. How many have nobly ascribed all recognized success and all avoidance of evil to the tenderness and devotion of mother. Through helpless infancy her throbbing heart was our strong support and safe protection. Through the ills of the day and the maladies of the night her gentle hand soothed as none other could. But, after all, this was mother's way.

Mother's Way

Sometimes when our hearts grow weary,
Or our task seems very long;
When our burdens look too heavy,
And we deem the right all wrong,
Then we gain a new, fresh courage,
As we rise to proudly say:
"Let us do our duty bravely,
This, you know, was mother's way."

• *Mothers are men-makers.* At a great public meeting of prominent men and women, one was introduced as a "self-made man." Instead of enjoying the tribute, it seemed to bother him. When later asked a reason, he replied, "Because I am not really a self-made man."

His friends insisted, "But did you not begin work in a store when you were only ten or twelve?"

"Yes," said he, "but it was because my mother thought I should start early to learn the educating touch of business."

"But then," they urged, "when you were a boy you were always an avid reader, devouring every book you could get."

"That is true," he replied, "but it was my mother who encouraged me to do it, and at her knee she had me give a report of the book after reading it."

They continued, "But your integrity is your own."

"Well, there was guidance. A barrel of apples came one day and I was to sell them. Following the manner of some storekeepers, I put the speckled ones at the bottom of each peck and the best ones on top. My mother called and asked what I was doing. I told her and she said, 'If you do that you will be a cheat'—and I did not do it. On the whole, I think my mother had much to do with making me. I am not self-made."

Blessed are those who had such a mother to exert a constructive influence over their formative years. And blessed is the mother who has a son or daughter so appreciative of her.

Really, the hand that rocks the cradle does more than rule the world, it also guides souls into the next one. How heavy is mother's responsibility! We live in a world of echoes; thus mothers must be careful what they speak. The weight of motherhood is greater than even mothers themselves can realize. But brave souls pulse on and victory rewards faith.

The Hand that Rocks the Cradle

They say that man is mighty,
He governs land and sea,
He wields a mighty scepter,
O'er lesser powers that be;
But a mightier power and stronger
Man from his throne has hurled,
For the hand that rocks the cradle
Is the hand that rules the world.

—WILLIAM ROSS WALLACE

4

My Mother

Who fed me from her gentle breast
And hushed me in her arms to rest,
And on my cheek sweet kisses prest?
    My mother.

When sleep forsook my open eye,
Who was it sung sweet lullaby,
And rocked me that I should not cry?
    My mother.

Who sat and watched my infant head
When sleeping in my cradle bed,
And tears of sweet affection shed?
    My mother.

When pain and sickness made me cry,
Who gazed upon my heavy eye
And wept, for fear that I should die?
  My mother.

Who ran to help me when I fell
And would some pretty story tell,
Or kiss the place to make it well?
  My mother.

Who taught my infant lips to pray,
To love God's Holy Word and day,
And walk in wisdom's pleasant way?
  My mother.

And can I ever cease to be
Affectionate and kind to thee
Who wast so very kind to me,
  My mother?

Oh, no, the thought I cannot bear;
And if God please my life to spare
I hope I shall reward thy care,
  My mother.

When thou art feeble, old and gray,
My healthy arm shall be thy stay,
And I will smooth thy pains away,
 My mother.

And when I see thee hang thy head,
'Twill be my turn to watch thy bed,
And tears of sweet affection shed—
 My mother!

—JANE TAYLOR

5

A Mother's Love

ONE OF THE MOST beautiful attributes of true and devoted motherhood is love. It describes a human tie which is gratefully acclaimed the world over as the greatest human love.

The love of husbands and wives may waver; brothers and sisters may become deep-rooted enemies; but a mother's love is so strong and unyielding that it usually endures all circumstances: good fortune and misfortune, prosperity and privation, honor and disgrace.

The only explanation for the unselfishness, sacrifice, loyalty and tenderness of motherhood is love.

What is love? The word is too big for any ordinary, brief definition. We can always turn to the dictionary, but in this case we are pondering a word much too meaningful for any dictionary to do it justice. But there is another book to which we can go for an analysis of love: the Bible. Ah, this is the book that tells us of love, that tells us of a word so big in sympathy, understanding and sacrifice that it was used to describe God: "God is love" (I John 4:8). So we now turn to the Holy Bible in search of a deeper understanding of a word which, when developed within a human heart, gives the person qualities which are Godlike.

The Bible gives a simple but marvelous analysis of love:

> *Love suffereth long, and is kind; love envieth not; love vaunteth not itself, is not puffed up, doth not behave itself unseemly, seeketh not its own, is not provoked, taketh not account of evil; rejoiceth not in unrighteousness, but rejoiceth with the truth; beareth all things, believeth all things, hopeth all things, endureth all things. Love never faileth.*
>
> —I Corinthians 13:4-8

• *Love is a refrainer.* "Love worketh no ill...," so declares the Bible. Negatively, love refrains from everything that would injure another. Love has a conscience. It penetrates into every aspect of life and abandons every thought which would do harm to others.

• *Love is a prompter.* Love will not be satisfied with a mere negative condition. It must work positive good. It opens man's heart in sympathy and stretches out the hand in helpfulness. Love endures the burning heat of summer and the icy frosts of winter, tarries in sick-rooms and lingers beside grave mounds, perils the blood and tears of battle-fields and binds up the wounds of fallen soldiers. Love is a compelling power.

An officer in the Confederate Army related in his Recollections a very touching story of a mother which illustrates the positive nature of love. On his way home after Appomattox, he saw a frail, hard-worked, withered woman wearing a faded calico dress and a common sunbonnet. She held the hand of a young man who had lost his sight from a wound received in battle. Even worse—the light of his mind was also gone. The mother had gone all the way from Texas to Virginia to take her blind and mindless boy back home. She brought him back sightless and mindless—but he was her son. It was a love that wars could not kill.

• *Another element of love is sacrificial energy.* Love gives of itself. In speaking of the love of Christ, the apostle Paul said, "…who loved me, and gave himself for me" (Galatians 2:20). This is love's behavior. Sacrifice is the very essence of love. It is not what we get, but what we give; and not in what we gain, but in what we are willing to lose.

A mother risks her life to bring her child into the world; and then gives herself little by little to see this new life blossom into maturity. This is mother's way.

Oftentimes mothers take risks far beyond the call of duty, risks which they should not take; but they do it because of the sacrificial quality of love which causes them to lose all thoughts of self and to center all thoughts upon the child.

A tragic incident in the royal family of England bears witness to this love. Years ago Mr. Gladstone, one of England's greatest premiers, walked into the English Parliament and stunned that august body with these solemn words: "Sires, Princess Alice is dead." Briefly, here are the circumstances. The princess' little baby had been sick with a contagious disease. The physicians had warned her not to touch the child. One day a nurse ran into the mother's room and said, "Princess Alice, your baby is dying." The princess rushed into the room and grabbed up the baby. The story can be concluded by noting that both were shortly buried in the same tomb.

While only a few mothers give their lives in a last and final act of devotion, yet mothers are legion who give themselves little by little in sacrificial services which spring from a deathless love for their children. They give and give and give.

Love's Prerogative

Love ever gives—
Forgives—outlives—
And ever stands
With open hands.
And while it lives—
   It gives
For this is love's prerogative—
   To give—and give—and give.

—JOHN OXENHAM

• *Love is tolerant.* "...love covereth a multitude of sins" (I Peter 4:8). It is not blind to faults, but sees them in the light of sympathy and affection.

When the wayward child is overcome by temptation, strays from the pathway of right, sinfully wanders into the gutter and is left there to die unnoticed and unaided by a cruel and heartless world, you may be sure that if his mother is living he still has a friend. That dear old mother will come and gather him up into her feeble arms and carry him home and tell him of all his virtues until he almost forgets that his soul was ever disfigured by vice. It is love which enables her to see him in a different light from the way the world views him.

• *Another ingredient of love is compassion.* That is beautifully exemplified in the very nature of God who is love. The Bible says this of him: "But thou, O Lord, art a God full of compassion, and gracious, long-suffering, and plenteous in mercy and truth" (Psalm 85:15). Because of compassion, God has remembered and blessed man.

When James A. Garfield was inaugurated President of the United States, March 4, 1881, he took the oath of office in the presence of a great throng, then he kissed the Holy Bible and turned and kissed the two women of his life: his aged mother and his wife. No artist can do that scene justice. A mother's love had prompted her to toil and care for him. She had led him in the ways of truthfulness and righteousness. The religious principles she had instilled in him had inspired him to do some preaching and to look upon the pulpit as the loftiest place to occupy. His comment was: "I step down out of the pulpit to become President of the United States."

Months rolled by and he became the victim of the assassin's bullet. During the long, weary weeks of suffering, he wrote but one letter and that was to his mother. He was acquainted with his mother's tears and prayers. He knew she wept and prayed for him. He knew every day was a long and anguished one for her.

"I must write mother," he said; and calling for pen and ink he wrote to her the only letter he penned after the assassin struck him down.

When Garfield's mother heard that he had been felled, she exclaimed from a mother's love, "Oh, why did they shoot my baby?" He was the President of the United States, but he was still to her, "My baby." This is love's way. This is mother's way.

• *Love is constant.* "Love never faileth" (I Corinthians 13:8). This is why a mother's feelings are not controlled by the cheers or jeers of a fickle crowd.

One of the most forceful and heroic examples of this stable love is seen at the crucifixion. It was a bloodthirsty crowd which watched Jesus die on that historic day. The Christ was so unpopular with the mob that they preferred Him to die in the place of Barabbas. His execution was turned into a mad circus. But His mother, with a broken and bleeding heart, stood among those haters and despisers of God that she might go with her Son as far as she could and comfort Him to the end. Jesus saw her in the crowd and made her earthly welfare one of His last cares. He commended her to the care of that disciple whom He loved so tenderly.

No finer compliment can be paid to womanhood than a recitation of the Biblical facts that women were among the last at the Cross, the first at the tomb on the day of our Lord's resurrection, and the first to greet the resurrected Savior (Matthew 27:55-28:10). This bears witness to a loyalty which cannot be excelled.

Mightiest Love

The name of mother! the sweetest name
That gently falls on mortal ear!
The love of mother! Mightiest love
Which Heaven permits to flourish here.

Dissect a mother's heart and see
The properties it doth contain—
What pearls of love, what gems of hope—
A mother's heart beats not in vain.

—CALEB DUNN

6

Rock Me to Sleep

Backward, turn backward,
  O time, in your flight!
Make me a child again, just for tonight!
Mother, come back from the echoless shore,
Take me again to your heart as of yore—
Kiss from my forehead the furrows of care,
Smooth the few silver threads out of my hair—
Over my slumbers your loving watch keep—
Rock me to sleep, mother—rock me to sleep!

Backward, flow backward, O tide of years!
I am so weary of toils and of tears—
Toil without recompense—tears all in vain—
Take them and give me my childhood again!
I have grown weary of dust and decay,

Weary of flinging my soul-wealth away—
Weary of sowing for others to reap;
Rock me to sleep, mother—rock me to sleep!

Tired of the hollow, the base, the untrue,
Mother, O mother, my heart calls for you!
Many a summer the grass has grown green,
Blossomed and faded—our faces between—
Yet with strong yearning and passionate pain,
Long I tonight for your presence again;
Come from the silence so long and so deep—
Rock me to sleep, mother—rock me to sleep!

Over my heart, in the days that are flown,
Your love, sweet mother-love, ever has shown—
No other service abides and endures,
Faithful, unselfish, and patient like yours.
None like a mother can charm away pain
From the sick soul and the world-weary brain;
Slumber's soft calm over my heavy lids creep—
Rock me to sleep, mother—rock me to sleep!

Come, let my brown hair, just lighted with gold,
Fall on your shoulders again as of old;
Let it fall over my forehead tonight,
Shielding my faint eyes away from the light;
For with its sunny-edged shadows once more
Hap'ly will throng the sweet visions of yore;
Lovingly, softly, its bright billows sweep—
Rock me to sleep, mother—rock me to sleep!

Mother, dear mother, the years have been long
Since I last hushed to your lullaby song;
Sing, then, and unto my soul it shall seem
Womanhood's years have been but a dream;
Clasped in your arms in a loving embrace,
With your light lashes just sweeping my face,
Never hereafter to wake or to weep—
Rock me to sleep, mother—rock me to sleep!

—ELIZABETH AKERS ALLEN

7

Mother and Prayer

MOTHER! O what a world of thoughts, like lightning, flash through the mind. What virtues of character warmed her soul and now shine upon ours. One of these was prayer, mother's prayer life. The echo of her prayers still falls gently upon our ears. As we reflect upon some of our earliest memories, we recall how mother taught us to pray, how she never tucked us in and kissed us goodnight without first insisting that we say our prayers.

• *Mothers know that we need someone bigger than ourselves* to whom we may freely go with our victories and defeats, joys and sorrows. That one is God, and the approach and conversation with Him is in prayer.

Every heart knows its own sorrow and every life has its own problems. In many a heart there abides a piercing pain of which the public knows very little. Fame, wealth and other symbols of success are often only the fruits of a diverted effort as a substitute for a peace we do not possess;

and are only the veneer which cover over our distressed souls. In the hours of trouble, when the help of man fails us, up goes our cry of anguish to God for sympathetic assistance.

Our many friends have understood its value. This is why they have so often said to us, "Remember me when you pray."

• *Mother had good reason to believe that prayer is necessary.* It is so essential that the Bible is filled with instructions on prayer. For our encouragement and help, hundreds of prayers are given in the Bible, many of which have recorded answers. Years of personal experience have taught us that we are too weak to lean on ourselves. Surely God wants us to lean heavily upon him in prayer. The person who has never availed himself of this blessed privilege is actually mistreating himself. Take time to pray.

Some Way

Somewhere, some way, some time each day,
I'll turn aside, and stop and pray
That God will bless me in the way,
As deeds I do and words I say.

• *Mother believed God has the ability and power to answer prayer.* This faith was based upon the teachings in the Holy Bible.

An ancient writer of Psalms said, "In my distress I cried

unto the Lord, and he heard me" (Psalm 120:1).

Jesus gave us these assurances: "If ye then, being evil, know how to give good gifts unto your children, how much more shall your Father which is in heaven give good things to them that ask him?" (Matthew 7:11). "And all things whatsoever ye shall ask in prayer, believing, ye shall receive" (Matthew 21:22). "If ye shall ask any thing in my name, I will do it" (John 14:14).

There is no problem our Father cannot solve; there is no heartache He cannot cure; there are no tears He cannot dry. God can deliver us from our distresses. Sometimes the deliverance frees us completely from the anguish; sometimes there is the alteration of the distress by which its agonizing pain is removed; and sometimes the deliverance comes in the form of God's giving us an abundant supply of grace which enables us to bear our burden patiently and heroically, discovering later that its presence encouraged a tenderness of heart and a richness of character. The latter was true of the apostle Paul who besought the Lord thrice to remove the thorn from his flesh. For his own good, God refused; but instead He gave him grace to bear it. In speaking of it, Paul said, "And he said to me, My grace is sufficient for thee: for my strength is made perfect in weakness. Most gladly therefore will I rather glory in my infirmities, that the power of Christ may rest upon me" (II Corinthians 3:19).

• *Prayer was never intended to encourage indolence,* God's laws were designed for the good of man. He wants us to do what we can for ourselves, and ask Him for the rest. This is true prayer. We pray, "Give us this day our daily bread," but we do not ask for it free from all effort on our part. Working for our sustenance is one of our blessings. God knew that and thus said, "In the sweat of thy face shalt thou eat bread till thou return unto the ground (Genesis 3:19).

God makes the sun to shine, the rain to fall, and the seed to sprout; but we must plow and sow and reap or our barns will remain empty. God hides the rocks in the mountains and covers the hills with trees; but we must quarry the rock, cut the timber, and put them in proper order or we will have no house for shelter. If we do, then we are workers together with God. Though God's part is infinitely bigger and more important than our part, both are necessary for the accomplishment of the divine purposes.

• *Our prayers should be real.* Ask no blessings you do not really want. Be honest in the expression of gratitude for the blessings you receive.

Our words of adoration and confidence should be absolutely sincere and true. Our speaking to God, filled with reverence and awe, should be as free as friend with friend. Praying should never be hurried over or done as an unpleasant task. Yet it need not necessarily be long, for we are not heard of God for our much speaking.

Ask God to give you strength to overcome your temptations. "Draw nigh to God, and he will draw nigh to you" (James 4:8). Jesus taught us to pray in the prayer of example: "And lead us not into temptation, but deliver us from evil." We need this help, for life has its sticky webs and ensnaring entanglements.

> *O thou child of many prayers!*
> *Life hath quicksands; life hath snares.*
>
> —HENRY W. LONGFELLOW

As a child of God, treasure His promises; ask in the name of Christ; be faithful, sincere, devout, and God will make His favor manifest in an untold number of ways. He will reward us openly.

• *We should be so grateful for our many blessings that we thank God for them.* "Every good gift and every perfect gift is from above, and cometh down from the Father of lights" (James 1:17). We are blessed every day in more than a thousand ways. We should learn to express our appreciation to both man and God for all their benefits. Ingratitude is one of the most despicable traits. In one of the longest and darkest list of sins given in the Bible we find this evil, "Because that, when they knew God, they glorified him not as God, neither were thankful" (Romans 1:21).

• *Many feel the need of mother's prayers,* even though she has been gone a long time. They knew she was on their side in life's struggles, and it meant so much to know they could count on her prayers. Their hearts have been lonely ever since she passed this life. If they could hear her pray again…what joy!

If I Could Hear My Mother Pray Again

How sweet and happy seems those days
    of which I dream,
When memory recalls them now and then!
And with what rapture sweet my weary heart
    would beat,
If I could hear my mother pray again.

If I could hear my mother pray again,
If I could hear her tender voice as then!
So glad I'd be, 'twould mean so much to me
If I could hear my mother pray again.

—J. W. VAUGHAN

8

A Priceless Mother

SOLOMON, the wise man, has laid down in the last chapter of Proverbs the sublime attributes of a priceless mother. He said, "Her price is far above rubies." Solomon's standard is high and exalted; but only by reaching upward to something above us can we elevate ourselves. Through the centuries this chapter has inspired good women, step by step, to plant their feet on higher ground.

There are blessings to be found in meditating upon Solomon's statements, verse by verse.

• *The worthy mother is invaluable.* "Who can find a virtuous [worthy, ASV] woman? for her price is far above rubies" (verse 10). No quantity of precious stones can equal her worth. There is no way to estimate correctly her true value. She is the foundation of the home; and the home is the foundation of civilization; so our world of tomorrow rests heavily upon mothers.

• *She is an efficient manager of the household.* "The heart of her husband doth safely trust in her, so that he shall have no need of spoil" (verse 11). Her husband has reason to trust her efficiency. He knows that where a person's heart is, there you will find that one's thoughts; so he is confident that his wife's thoughts are first, last and always centered around the welfare of the home.

Since women spend most of the money in the family budget, then it is important that mothers be good managers. There are two ways families can become rich without increasing their income: wisely handle what they have, and secondly, decrease their wants. The wise mother knows that happiness comes not from what you have, but from what has you.

• *The worthy mother is good to her husband.* "She will do him good and not evil all the days of her life" (verse 12). It is easy for her to be good, because she is good. All she has to do to be good is to be in character. Her goodness is unmixed—"she will do him good and not evil." We have observed that good people are good to all; and evil people are evil to all, even to their own children when selfish interests are involved.

• *She works willingly.* "She seeketh wool, and flax, and worketh willingly with her hands" (verse 13). She seeks the necessary materials for her family's clothing. She finds joy in this service to her loved ones. All her services are rendered cheerfully; and we do not have to guess why—her heart is in it. Willing work contributes to a pleasant and happy family; on the other hand, duties performed grudgingly and bitterly spread a cloud of despondency and depreciation over the family circle.

• *She is ingenious.* "She is like the merchants' ships; she bringeth her food from afar" (verse 14). She is resourceful like the merchants who send out their ships. She brings her food from afar, taking advantage of bargains and terms. This takes planning, but she gladly does it for the benefit of her family. Caring for her household is not on a momentary, haphazard basis; but, instead, she thinks about their future and plans for their good.

• *In her wise management, she plans for increased holdings.* "She considereth a field, and buyeth it: with the fruit of her hands she planteth a vineyard" (verse 16). She provides for the growing needs of her family. As the family increases, more facilities will be needed. Her prudence and economy enhance the family's assets. She wants her household to be independent and self-reliant; so she plants a vineyard that their crops may increase. Fortunate are the children whose parents instill in them the feeling of self-reliance, which causes them to look to themselves and to God for their wants. This spirit is their strongest security.

• *With energy and force she prepares herself for her work.* "She girdeth her loins with strength, and strengtheneth her arms" (verse 17). This is a metaphorical statement. Metaphorically speaking, strength and vigor are the girdle she binds around her waist which enables her to carry out her duties. Through her own thinking she has added firmness to her loins and strength to her arms. She is not self-defeated through thinking she is weak; but, instead, she has added to her vitality by thinking she is strong. Certainly there are limitations; but, to an extent, as we think we are, we are. Solomon said, "For as he thinketh in his heart, so is he" (Proverbs 23:7).

• *The excellent mother has busy and exemplary hands.* She layeth her hands to the spindle, and her hands hold the distaff" (verse 19). Since Solomon wrote this chapter, the type of work has changed; but the need for work will remain with us forever. The efficient mother's chief concern is not to have pretty hands, but useful hands. She is not a manager only; she is also a worker. She knows that the best way to teach her children to work is by example; so by inspiration and perspiration she brings out the best in them. She sets the pace and others in the household follow. She knows that working does not lessen her feminine qualities, but enhances personal dignity and self-respect. She finds happiness in work. In contrast, others find misery in idleness.

• *She is sympathetic and charitable.* "She stretcheth out her hand to the poor; yea, she reacheth forth her hands to the needy" (verse 20). Having a good and unselfish heart, it is as natural for her to extend helpful and benevolent hands to the poor and needy as it is for a good tree to bear good fruit. Her ministering hands reach beyond her family, for they can stretch as far as opportunity permits; and opportunities are not hard to find, if one has the heart for them.

She gives because her heart is big; and in dividing her blessings, she multiplies her own happiness and contentment.

• *Having made preparation, she faces the future unafraid.* "She is not afraid of the snow for her household: for all her household are clothed with scarlet" (verse 21). Winter brings no fears, for she is prepared for it. She uses the summer days to prepare for the wintry blasts sure to come. Following day, comes the night; and following sunshine, comes the rain; and following summer, comes the winter. It is a known fact that life has its adversities; so we should exercise enough industry and maturity to make preparation for the trying circumstances. They will come, prepared or unprepared.

• *Her household is comfortably furnished and her body is properly adorned.* "She maketh herself coverings of tapestry; her clothing is silk and purple" (verse 22). As a well balanced person, she does something for others and something for self. This is life at its best. For her guests, she makes tapestry as carpeting for them to sit upon and quilted work for the beds. For herself, she makes clothing of silk and purple. The deserving mother dresses herself in keeping with good taste, avoiding the two extremes of homely unattractiveness and expensive extravagance.

• *She is a source of respectability and honor for her husband.* "Her husband is known in the gates, when he sitteth among the elders of the land" (verse 23). The citizens respect him because of his neatness and cleanliness of dress, but most of all because he is the husband of a woman known for her good works and devotion to her husband and children. Her expert management of his home enables him to devote time to personal business and to the welfare of the community. She is truly a help meet, or a co-worker with her husband. Every man needs this kind of help.

• *She adds to the family income.* "She maketh fine linen, and selleth it; and delivereth girdles unto the merchant" (verse 24). Perhaps she never had a course in economics, but she understands the importance of adding a little extra money to the family purse. It is evident that she is willing to bear her share of the home load and then some.

• *The meritorious mother's most beautiful wardrobe is moral and spiritual and consists of garments for the soul.* "Strength and honor are her clothing; and she shall rejoice in time to come" (verse 25). Such clothing is not always popular, but is always respected; and it makes for self-respect and dignity.

• *Her speech is wise and uplifting.* "She openeth her mouth with wisdom; and in her tongue is the law of kindness" (verse 26). There is an explanation of such wise and kind speech: it is in the heart. Jesus explained: "For out of the abundance of the heart the mouth speaketh" (Matthew 12:34). So each needs to "Keep thy heart with all diligence; for out of it are the issues of life" (Proverbs 4:23). The intelligent and kind mother guides her family with appropriate words. When she talks, it is not filthy vulgarity, degrading gossip or assassinating slander. Her speech is filled with prudence and good sense, regulated by love, free from vindictiveness and hate.

• *The praiseworthy mother exercises loving surveillance over the conduct in the family.* "She looketh well to the ways of her household, and eateth not the bread of idleness" (verse 27). She is a moral and spiritual supervisor. She sees that all behave themselves well, shunning bad company and immoral habits. She has lived long enough and observed enough to know that "evil companionships corrupt good morals."

She eats not the bread of idleness, for she knows that is wrought with many vices. Every person in the family needs a job. We are somewhat like a shovel in that we are not so apt to wear out through work as we are to rust out through inactivity.

• *She has the respect of her husband and children.* "Her children arise up, and call her blessed; her husband also, and he praiseth her" (verse 28). The ones who know her best, her husband and children, who have the broadest opportunities to see her under all circumstances, are unanimous in their praise of her. She has their approbation, because she has earned it. They have been the objects of her affectionate care, and now they reciprocate by praising and blessing her.

• *She is the incomparable wife and mother who excels them all.* "Many daughters have done virtuously, but thou excellest them all" (verse 29). This undoubtedly is the husband's testimony to the excellence of his wife. Many have acted with due propriety, but she outstrips them all.

Through greater and wiser service, she has become a greater mother. Jesus said, "But he that is greatest among you shall be your servant" (Matthew 23:11).

• *The noble mother has a deep and unfading beauty.* "Favor is deceitful, and beauty is vain: but a woman that feareth the Lord, she shall be praised" (verse 30). Manners may be deceitful. A pleasing personality may be feigned in an effort to hide the true nature. A fair appearance may be learned by mere physical discipline and will continue as long as the restraint lasts; but it is only hypocrisy, veneer, an outward semblance. It is all outside show; and having nothing within to produce it, the make-believe finally becomes too heavy for itself and drops.

"Beauty is vain." Perfection of shape, dignity of features and smoothness of skin are all vanity. Suffering impairs them; age changes them; and death destroys them. But the woman who fears the Lord shall be praised. Her consecration to the Lord cools her temper, purifies her soul and gives her a lasting beauty, for it is within her.

• *Her own works praise her.* "Give her of the fruit of her hands; and let her own works praise her in the gates" (verse 31). She has the right to enjoy the fruit of her hands. She has sown industry, zeal, economy, prudence and righteousness; and now it is only fair that she reap these blessings.

A Worthy Mother

Gentle hands that never weary of toiling in
    love's vineyard sweet.
Eyes that seem forever cherry when our eyes
    they chance to meet.
Tender, patient, brave, devoted—this is
    always mother's way.
Could her worth in gold be quoted as you
    think of her today?

There shall never be another quite so tender,
    quite so kind
As the patient little mother;
    no where on this earth you'll find
Her affection duplicated;
    none is quite so fine.
Could her worth be overstated?
    Not by any words of mine.

Vain are all our tributes to her,
  if in words alone they dwell.
We must live the praises due her.
  There's no other way to tell
Gentle mother that we love her.
  Would you say, as you recall
All the patient service of her
  that you've been worthy of it all?

9

The Brave Mother

*E*VERY STRONG and influential mother has courage as a basic element of character. Fearlessness is a quality of the heart. It is a dynamic power within us that controls our behavior as we face difficulties, trials and danger. It does not depend on what we have but rather on what we are.

Physical courage is seen as a person risks life for another or a cause. The soldier who gives his life for his country is honored among the nation's heroes; but we often forget the heroism of those who live and serve and die a little every day in the home.

Years ago at the outbreak of World War II, the railway stations were crowded with families bidding good-bye to those who were being inducted into military service. Brokenhearted wives were saying good-bye to their husbands. Sisters were parting from brothers, many of them never to see each other again on this earth. Sweethearts were embracing lovers as if they could not turn loose.

Mothers with bleeding hearts, tearful but brave, followed their sons as far as the eye could see. It was a time in which the hearts of women as well as men were being tried to the utmost, and those women reached down into the bottom of their hearts and found a bravery the whole world admires.

The Brave at Home

The mother who conceals her grief
 When to her breast her son she presses,
Then breathes a few brave words and brief,
 Kissing the patriot brow she blesses,
With no one but her secret God
 To know the pain that weighs upon her,—
Sheds brave blood as e'er the sod
 Received on freedom's field of honor.

—THOMAS R. READ

Moral courage is witnessed by a person's willingness to stand for his convictions against opposition, unpopularity and persecution. The world is filled with weak people who are willing to stand where there is no testing and who are willing to back a friend when he really needs no backing. But only the brave will stand when it is unpopular.

It is the bravest kind of courage to face the everyday affairs of life. It is on this battlefield that mothers display a heroic nature that is unexcelled. It is here that they unflinchingly triumph amid all the opposition and friction, strain and heartbreak of life.

• *Mothers have to fight hard, but they gain immensely from the struggle.* Character is strengthened by facing difficulties and overcoming them. The struggle develops fortitude. Every victory won fits the victor to win another.

One of the blessings from life's trials is that only those who have been brave enough to struggle can know rest and calm.

> *He who hath never a conflict,*
> *hath never a victor's palm.*
> *And only the toilers know the sweetness*
> *of rest and calm.*

Victory and peace across over in heaven will be all the sweeter because of the struggles on earth through which we must pass to win them.

• *The universal need for mothers with all their attendant services has compelled them to become creatures of bravery.* The need is so great they cannot afford to be otherwise.

A young schoolteacher said, "No, I can't go anywhere this vacation. You know, I'm the eldest daughter and when I'm out of school there are so many things for me to do. Mother isn't very strong and the children are always needing things."

Her friend, older by several years, watched her as she

went from one task to another. "Oh, you fortunate girl," breathed the friend with a warm smile. "I don't know whether you realize it or not, but the most blessed thing in all the world is to be needed."

Oh, the blessedness of being needed!

• *A strong faith makes a person brave.* Our faith guards us against fainting with fear as it protected the Psalmist, who said, "I had fainted, unless I had believed to see the goodness of the Lord in the land of the living" (Psalm 27:13). His faith gave him courage to say, "I will fear no evil: for thou art with me…" (Psalm 23:4).

What though a thousand hosts engage
A thousand worlds my soul to shake!
I have a shield that shall quell the rage,
Portrayed, a precious promise heard.
'Twill drive the alien armies back—
I dare believe in God's good word.

It is faith which has given mothers the valiant nobility to accept disappointment as a new appointment.

God's Appointment

Dis-appointment—His appointment;
Change one letter, then I see
That the thwarting of His purpose
Is God's better plan for me.

What a person thinks, does, determines, when things are at their worst, makes or mars that person's future. Bitter disappointment, broken trust, the fading of cherished hopes, precipitate a crisis for every soul thus tried; for it is then that the soul must choose hate, bitterness, and despair—or else have the courage to choose the way of forgiveness, toil and perseverance.

• *Assurance imbues the heart of mother with valor.* She has the unqualified assurance that she, as a mother, is a partner with God in perpetuating man whom the Father created. She has the certainty that in nourishing and training the child she holds in her hand the power to mold future civilization. She feels that God would not put such responsibility upon a mortal without giving some assistance, and she believes that she has it. This assurance makes her strong. "We are more than conquerors through him that loved us" (Romans 8:37).

This assurance brightens her eyes; it quickens her pulse; it strengthens her arms; it kindles the love of her soul. It makes her throb with aspiration, work with diligence, twinkle with enthusiasm, melt with pity, glow with joy and soar with rapture.

Assurance—it makes her a heroine!

> *The greatest battle that ever was fought—*
> *Shall I tell you where and when?*
> *On the maps of the world you will find it not:*
> *It was fought by the mothers of men.*
>
> —Joakuin Miller

10

A Prayer for Mothers

OUR FATHER which art in heaven, we are grateful that Thou hast given the world mothers, the torchbearers of life, the foundation of civilization. We thank Thee for our own dear mothers who bore us in travail and loved us all the more for the pain we brought; who suffered for us in body, mind and soul; who gave us a warm feeling of security by their tireless sacrifices and undying devotion; for the agony with which they watched over us in sickness and nursed us back to health; for the sorrow that pierced their hearts when we were foolish; for the smiles of appreciation and joy that played across their faces when we achieved some little accomplishment; for the thousand little tasks they performed daily to make life better for others.

Dear God, if we have been selfish and thoughtless and have taken the fruit of their labors as our due without showing appreciation, forgive us this sin.

Our Father, we beg of Thee to bless all the good women who are now bearing the weariness and pain of maternity. Give them strength of body and courage of mind for their new responsibilities. Grant them the vision to see themselves not in the limited role of mother of one child or several, but rather in the larger role as patriot women who hold in their hands the future of our civilization.

We pray that sober and wholesome influences may be thrown around the girls of today that they may be impressed with the importance of their future calling, and that they may preserve their bodies and minds in strength and purity for the lofty occupation to which the future may summon them.

Righteous Father, bestow Thy tenderness on all worthy women who have maternal yearnings but whose lives are barren of its joys; who have a mother's heart but feel the ache of empty arms...help them to overcome the disappointment and dismay...may they find an outlet for their thwarted mother-instinct as they exert the sweet ministries of motherhood in the family circle and as they touch the lives of the lonely and unmothered wherever they may be.

Bless all mothers, we pray Thee, who have suffered the unsurpassed sorrow of having their own children taken from them in death and now must heroically press onward in life's duties, destitute of one of its sweetest joys...dry up their tears and heal their aching hearts.

And for us we pray, our Father, that the hallowed memories of such illustrious mothers may lift us to higher living…may we live the praises due them. In Christ's name. Amen.

When God thought of mother,
He must have laughed with satisfaction,
and framed it quickly—
so rich, so deep, so divine,
so full of soul, power, and beauty,
was the conception.

—HENRY WARD BEECHER